Understanding Musicality

Dinámica y Sincopación

Filling in the Blanks of Argentine Tango

- Book Six -

Oliver Kent PhD

Finding Hope : Searching for Happiness Book 1

Opening to Love : Healing Your Relationship With God

Illustrations by Oscar B Frise

Dedicated to Kätzchen, for everything.

Table of Contents

About the Author

Oliver Kent has been dancing all his life and Argentine Tango for longer than he can remember. He's noticed that there are a lot of "blanks" in the way tango is usually taught that you're supposed to fill in by dancing socially. Unfortunately this doesn't always work that well and many find themselves making slow progress, or stuck on a plateau.

Oliver's experience and ability to coherently explain these details is regularly sought out by dancers from all over the world, from those just getting their feet wet, to established teachers.

He originally intended to write a book filling in the blanks, enabling others to become good social dancers. He then realized he'd underestimated just how many blanks there were! The book became a trilogy, which in turn became a series.

Referring to Previous Books in the Series

It's surprising just how many Blanks there are to Fill in for becoming a Good Social Dancer! Although I realize some will read these books out of order or only read a few of them, they are intended to be read as a series.

Each book builds on the next.

If you can't actually get any dances, then everything else is academic. Hence the first book focuses on this. A good tango posture and embrace makes actual dancing so much easier – this is covered in Books 2 and 3.

And then ideally, you need to be able to lead and/or follow in a connected, comfortable way that allows you to move freely – the topic of this and future books.

To avoid repeating massive amounts of previous

books, I will simply refer to them in the text like this (Book 1.)

You don't need to have read any of my other books in order to use this one. If you're content that you have a good social embrace already – or that the one you have is good enough for now – then you can certainly use that for practicing the ideas in this book.

My intention is to write in a way that if you have read my other books you'll gain extra insight; not to make parts of the book inaccessible if you haven't.

Music

Although pictures help, there's no real substitute for being able to hear music.

Regarding tango music, in the US, after 50 years music enters the Public Domain and loses its copyright status. Given that 95% of tango music was written before 1950, that's most of it. Certainly everything I've referred to in this book.

Generally, searching for the artist and the song on YouTube will find you the track. You can also buy the songs from "all good music stores" either digitally or, if you have something that will play them, on cds and even records!

All material referenced in this book is done so under Fair Use for Educational Purposes. No infringement of copyright is intended or should be implied. I categorically don't own any of these works.

A brief note on the illustrations

The illustrations in this book are there to guide you through each step, enabling you to build an embrace which, like a custom fitted suit, fits you perfectly and is unique to you. As such, they're illustrative rather than prescriptive.

None of these illustrations are intended to be something that you copy exactly. If a paragraph asks you to move the follower's right hand down, don't worry about the precise angle the model's knee is at.

A quick overview of moves

While this is no means an extensive list of tango moves - to aid the flow of the book - I'm going to give a brief explanation of some. While each has a lot of variations, this is enough for these purposes.

These are intended for you if don't know these moves, so don't worry. I refer to them in the book, but you won't need to actually be able to do them yet. Any teacher or experienced dancer will be able to demonstrate these moves in a few seconds, if you ask them nicely.

Free and Weighted Legs

The "free leg" is the one you aren't standing on. Whereas, the "weighted leg" is the one you are standing on.

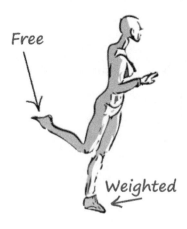

Open and Closed-side

The open-side is the one where you (usually) hold hands.

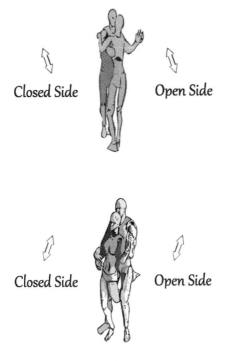

Closed Side   Open Side

Closed Side   Open Side

Boleo (boh-LAY-oh)

A graceful arcing movement of the free leg.

Cuddle-shuffling

Dancing only using weight-changes and shuffling around. Usually done in close embrace - an effective way to accelerate your progress (Book 3)

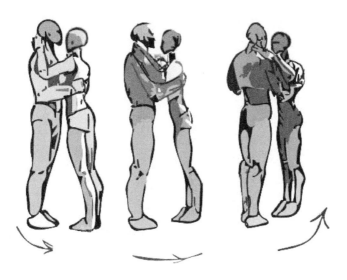

xxx

Introduction

"Why should you even learn about musicality?"

Some consider themselves Free Spirits and are quite proud that they have no idea about the music;

"I just dance" they happily reply.

Others respond to these Free Spirits by quoting Nietzsche, who wasn't terribly impressed with their position:

'And those who could not hear the music were insane to consider themselves dancing'

But in doing so they miss the point. Free Spirits are usually simply enjoying themselves and more importantly, they want to enjoy themselves. They're more focused either on the pleasure of dancing, or enjoying creating things spontaneously.

They're not looking for a Big Book of Techniques, or The Right Way to do Things.

Other people want to accumulate knowledge. They want to understand musicality so they can be better dancers, but they view it rather like a test to be passed. For them it's important to know how many beats are in a bar, the difference between a bandoneon and an accordion, and not only the orchestra that is being played, but who the singer is and decade it's from.

They want to be able to give an informed opinion on whether Biagi was better before, or after, he split from D'Arienzo. And they want to know who Biagi and D'Arienzo were!

Somewhere in-between, are people just want to dance without appearing foolish. If everyone seems to know who DiSarli is, they'd quite like to know too. But they're not going to worry about going beyond that point.

And of course there are those who Bluff and Expound with Great Importance, because that's what makes them feel happy, or at least, less embarrassed.

All these things have their place in tango.

But for this book we're going to start by looking at how you can use musicality to enhance your social dancing. Beginning with the questions you may be too embarrassed to ask, through to understanding how tango music works.

Then gradually building up to being able to hear cues in the music so you don't need to do calculus while you dance.

Quick refresher

Before we get started, there's a few things that I'm going to assume you know, going into this book.

The Compás of a song is the underlying beat or rhythm. For tango it's usually around 120 Beats Per Minute (BPM), or two beats every second.

The odd beats are sometimes more accentuated that the even ones.

In order to do a graceful tango walk to a song with a Compás of 120 BPM, you either:

• Take smaller steps. Realistically this means at least halving the length of your stride. You may find doing it on tip-toes helps too.

• Or you can step on every odd beat, collecting (bringing your feet together) on the even ones.

Also for this book I'm going to continue to make use of the idea that groups of 8 beats can be important and refer to them as One through Eight, accordingly.

Troubleshooting

If you're not confident with the above, I recommend spending more time working on the exercises in the previous book.

Ok, onto the new stuff!

Chapter 1 Double Time

"In my point of view, tango is, above all, rhythm, nerve, strength and character. Early tango, that of the Old Guard, had all that, and we must try not to ever lose it."

- Juan D'Arienzo

You may have noticed that tango dancers like to name things – there's an entire section at the beginning of this book just dealing with terminology and another one at the end– and this is no exception.

Terminology – Normal time

The baseline for tango – roughly one step per second.

Terminology – Double time

If you're going "twice as fast" as a normal tango walk it's called "Double time." - roughly two steps per second and walking on each beat of the

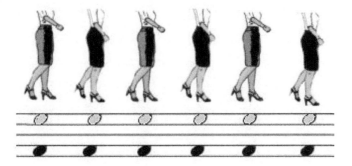

But why "double-time" rather than "half-time"? After all, in order to walk at double time, the steps are half as long.

If you get confused, remember that tango dancers stole a lot of musicality concepts from musicians and butchered them in the process. Musicians are only concerned about how fast they're playing, not how long your steps are!

So double time = twice as fast.

Problems

"Warp speed Mr Sulu!" ~ *Captain James T Kirk*

There are two common problems with double-time.

A lot of leaders believe they have the choice of

either leading a walk at double-time, or using a specific move, often a giro or cross.

Let's start with leading a double-time walk.

Generally to dance at that speed, you can either "shuffle", taking steps that are half as big (and so only take half as long to complete) or just weight change.

Instead, most leader's attempt double-time walks with their normal length stride, making their life a lot harder than it needs to be. It tends to be more like the Secret Service getting the President to safety, rather than a graceful tango walk.

Leader's also quickly recognize that if it doesn't work, there's a pretty good chance you'll, at best, step on the follower's feet. At worst, you'll fall over them as they don't move back fast enough.

You also need quite a bit of room to do this. If you need to keep taking three steps every time you need to do a double-time, you'll probably find the dancers in front of you are getting in your way.

Ok, so what about the cross and the giro?

They're generally taught as part of a sequence. In fact, many leaders chose a specific sequence that they find works best for them and tend to stick to it.

But this means it now takes time to go through

the sequence to get to the double-time step. If you know the music well, you can start sufficiently ahead of time. But this causes further problems.

The clearest example of this is when, sooner or later, a dancer learns the concept of a "dramatic finish move." In Argentine Tango, it might mean ending the song in a lunge. These tend to suffer from the same problem – the leader needs to work out how early to start the sequence to hit the end with the "cool move."

If you watch social dancers do this, you'll see a marked shift from dancing to "thinking / planning ahead." The dancing leading up to the final sequence gets clunkier as the leader stops focusing on the moment.

Similarly, if you need to keep planning ahead every time you want to lead a double-time, it will mess up your dancing. And your follower will feel your connection shifting from them to "planning."

I've seen leaders try to solve the problem by leading a giro to get to double-time and then just staying there for the rest of the dance. The phrase "Bull in a china shop" was repeatedly used by the other leaders who were less than pleased to be sharing the floor with a small hurricane, taking full-length steps at double time and zooming around.

This is why I recommend learning musicality with Cuddle-shuffling. You can react to changes in the music immediately – there's no sequences to get through. And you can either shuffle around with small steps without annoying anyone around, or even just weight-change in place if there's no space at all.

Trouble-shooting

You will occasionally run into people who argue that double-time should mean "twice as slow" and half-time, "twice as fast." Given that the tango police don't (officially) exist, this isn't really a problem as long as you both understand what the other person means.

What is Syncopation anyway?

Again, at the risk of upsetting musicians, as far as social tango dancers are concerned syncopation, or sincopación, is simply when you're not marching to the beat. Specifically, when you're not dancing to the odd beats.

Terminology: Sincopación

When you're not marching to the beat.

Double-time is a sincopación because it involves dancing to the even beats.

Summary

- Normal time: The baseline for tango – roughly one step per second.

- Double time: If you're going "twice as fast" as a normal tango walk it's called "Double time." - roughly two steps per second and walking on each beat of the Compás.

- Learning to do double-time as part of a walk or sequence is problematic.

- Practicing with Cuddle-shuffling is much easier.

- Sincopación is when you're not marching to the odd beats.

- Double-time is a sincopación because it involves dancing to the even beats.

Chapter 2 Mixing it Up

"Hey, Hey! What's this I see? I thought this was a party? LET'S DANCE!"

- Footloose

I vividly remember the confusion double-time first caused me. You can hear it in the music, but then that opens up all sorts of questions -

When do you do it? Do you have to do it? Do you have to mark all the double-times? What's the best way?

Short answers -

• It depends on who you ask. (No, really - there's big disagreement on this in the Argentine Tango community.)

• Ideally when there's an actual double-time in the music.

- Nope. You are the master of your own destiny. Unless you're following, in which case, your leader can strongly suggest it to you. Even then, you can still sometimes choose to dance the double-time by adding extra steps or taps.

- Definitely don't feel obliged to do double-time, or to do it for any longer than you want to. If you want to mark a long phrase in the music with just one double-time step, or indeed none, that's your choice.

- There's a few, which we'll get into throughout this book.

Having the freedom to change between dancing at the full BPM (double-time) and half the BPM (normal-time), whenever you want, opens up a lot of musicality options for you as a social tango dancer.

To start with, let's get used to moving between using normal time and double-time.

Exercise 1

Search YouTube for "Metronome 120 BPM."

Switch back and forth between clapping to all the beats and every second one.

When you're confident, repeat but change between shuffling to the full BMP and walking to the half speed version, for example:

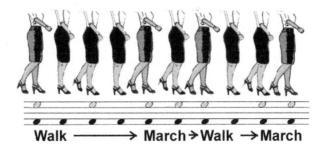

Walk ⟶ March → Walk → March

Again the above is just one possibility. Experiment with other variations.

Trouble-shooting

To walk at double-time, halve the length of your steps. You can make them even smaller if that's easier.

Don't rush this stage.

For social dancing you'll want to be able to do

this without having to think about it. At first you may find you need to take a mental "run-up" - it feels a lot like when you were a child and were learning how to step onto an escalator. You can clap as well, if that makes it easier.

When you can do this without thinking, if you're a follower, now you need to do this walking backwards. I'd recommend you start in flats until you can do it without thinking and only then put on heels, if you dance in them.

Putting it all-together

One of the biggest traps of social tango dancing is having too much going on in your head.

"I need to do this and this and this and this and...!"

The series is deliberately written to minimize the amount you need to think about while dancing. Looking over the previous books, first you get your posture sorted out before you ask someone to dance. Then focus on what you need to do to get the dances you want.

Once you've got one, you can stop thinking about it. Your posture is already good so you don't need to think about that. Use the Introduction of the music to embrace and tune into your partner and what the music has in store. Then you can stop thinking about what you need to do for your embrace too.

Now focus on your partner and the musical cues in the moment. If you're using a combination of walking and shuffling, you don't need to be thinking about sequences either.

Just dance.

Of course, you have to enjoy things and the above isn't everyone's cup of tea, so if you want to throw in some moves, go ahead.

But I still recommend doing the above some of the time - you'll progress a lot faster if you don't have your head filled with moves and sequences, especially if you can't quite do them yet.

The nice thing about the musicality in this book is you can get a lot of mileage on your own. You can shuffle around at home or even do it on the subway, just subtly tapping your hand or foot.

Which leads us to:

The Big Secret of Musicality

"Musicality is about patterns. And your brain is really good at finding patterns."

For any concept you read in this book, if you put on a piece of music that contains it and just try to move to it, your brain will start figuring it out. It might take a few minutes, an hour, a day, a week. But just let your subconscious do what it does and it will start to come together.

This is the inherent beauty of tango.

This book is pretty much just about showing your brain what it's looking for and then you just have to play around with it.

To read the above paragraph, you didn't have to find the "One", work out how many "counts" there were, consider which section it was, or the relationships between the words and so on.

You just did it.

The other benefit of this is that "good" music for social dancing follows these patterns. But every now and then you'll dance to something that really should have be enjoyed by sitting down with a glass of wine.

The benefit of using this approach, is that even if the song does something strange, both you and your partner will likely make the same "mistake." For example, the song ends abruptly a beat early, but you both take one more step.

For a competition, this would be a problem, but for social dancing, just smile – your partner will probably do the same.

Summary

- Ideally don't dance double-time if it's not in the music.

- If it is in the music, you still don't have to dance it.

- To walk at double-time, halve the length of your steps. You can make them even smaller if that's easier.

- "Musicality is about patterns. And your brain is really good at finding patterns."

Chapter 3 Half time

"If there is no beat, there is no tango."

~ *Juan D'Arienzo*

In Book 5, I explained how some dancers mainly hear the rhythm, some the lyrics and some the melody, with a few hearing more than one.

A similar thing applies to the speed at which you're comfortable dancing at. Some dancers like to go fast and will lose their balance if you go slowly. Others prefer to go slowly and start to trip over themselves if you go fast. Take a guess which end of the spectrum a friend nicknamed "Tazmanian Devil" is at?

And some just prefer the music to be "just right." Goldilocks would have loved the Argentine Tango.

I once did this as an experiment at a Práctica.

I'd been trying out the different Dinámica over

the past few weeks there and noticed that it was much easier to lead some on certain followers than others. To test my theory, I brought along several songs – each one suited a different Dinámic. I matched each song to a specific follower and got a friend to film me dancing.

I was astonished to see how much the dances differed from each-other. Each dance was a dream to lead.

I then briefly attempted to get the followers to dance to the tracks that didn't suit them. That was a train wreck and I quickly gave up on it!

Slowing things down

"Dancing slower" usually means "Half time" in Argentine Tango - moving at half normal speed, usually one step every two seconds.

Terminology – Half time

As double-time is twice as fast, "half time" is half as fast.

You can accomplish this by stepping on every fourth beat of the Compás: if you step on the One, your next step would be on the Five.

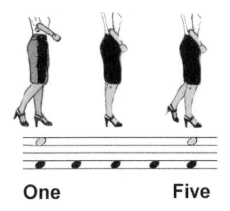

One   **Five**

If you started on the Three, your next step would be on the Seven and so on.

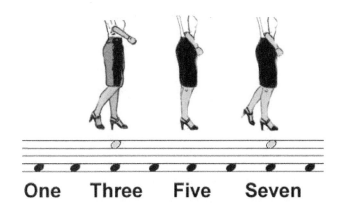

One   **Three**   **Five**   **Seven**

Troubleshooting

While it still works, the maths starts to get

troublesome when you go past Eight.

Consider this sentence for a moment.

"Using Half-time, if you step on the Seven, then your next step is on the Three."

It's right. And it makes more sense visually

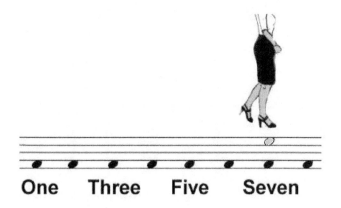

One   Three   Five   Seven

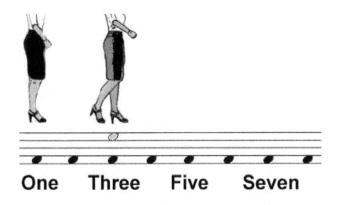

One   Three   Five   Seven

But said out-loud it's just confusing to most. This is another reason I'm not fond of counting beats for any longer than you have to.

"Step at half-speed" is much easier than

"Ok, I'm on the Seven. Eight minus seven is one; four minus one is three. Right, I need to step on the Three next!"

Also by the time you've worked that out, you've probably missed the Three anyway...

Dancing at half-time takes a lot more skill. Again a reason I much prefer cuddle-shuffling for learning this. It's much easier to balance and there's a lot less going on and demanding your attention.

Trouble-shooting

Although there is a logic to it, you don't need your stride to be twice as long for half-time. Your normal stride is fine. Likewise you can still do half-time with smaller steps and even weight-changes. Although it's a style choice, I'd strongly recommend keeping your free foot lightly in contact with the ground if you do this.

If you've ever ridden the subway, you'll know that even making light contact with a handrail will drastically improve your balance. Similarly, having both your feet in contact with the ground is much easier to balance in, than only one.

Just as you can also deliberately step on the even beats for normal (Two, Four, Six, Eight), you can also do this for half time (Two and Six, or Four and Eight), though this will feel strange.

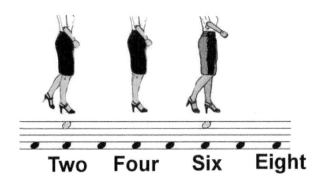

Two   Four   Six   Eight

Unfortunately, tango music doesn't really lend itself to playing long sections of half-time.

You can practice to either:

120 BPM (Step on every fourth beat)

60 BPM metronome (step on every second beat)

30 BPM metronome (step on every beat)

You'd think it would be easiest to use the 30 BPM version – after all there's no extra maths involved. The problem is that when you try, it's actually quite tricky to gauge exactly when you're supposed to step. Stepping once or twice a second is pretty straight-forward.

But oddly, once every two seconds is a lot harder. If you want to try it to music, "Jazzchains" by The Deli, has a nice, consistent half-time (for tango) beat.

Ok, so that probably doesn't work so well.

Fortunately, in tango, the Compás provides you with extra signposts.

Exercise 2

Search for "60 BPM metronome." Walk to it using half-time.

Rather than thinking of the 60 BPM as stepping on every second beat, think of it as "step, collect, step, collect" to the beat.

Now try it to Andrew Strong's version of "Mustang Sally."

It's doable, but you should now feel why no-one really walks in half-time for any length of time.

Exercise 3

When you're comfortable with a half-time walk,

now's the time to try it to a 120 BPM metronome.

Trouble-shooting

You might need to go back and forth between the 120 and 60 BPM metronomes while your brain and body have a discussion on how this is going to work. Don't rush things. Check that you've got a good tango posture – when you're concentrating on one specific thing, it can be easy to unconsciously change back to the way you habitually stand. (For more information on tango posture see Book 2.)

You can also choose to pause for a moment longer when you collect, to regain your balance, before continuing with the exercise. Also there's nothing wrong with having your hand against a wall for extra balance, while you get more skilled at doing this.

Exercise 4

Canaro's Poema, though a little slow, is a good song to practice to.

For normal time, just walk "step, collect, step" on the beat with a normal-sized tango walk.

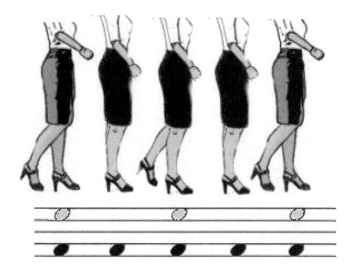

For double time, step on each beat - use a smaller step, "shuffle" or weight change.

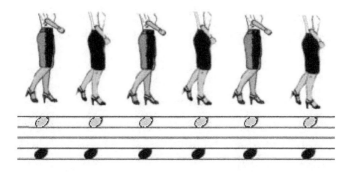

To practice half-time, skip ahead to the vocals.

The time between when he pauses and when he starts to sing again is a half-time step. Definitely start with a normal-sized tango walk for this.

Then try smaller steps, shuffles and weight-changes when you feel confident.

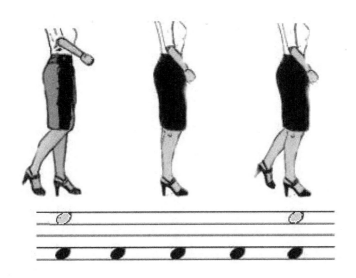

Trouble-shooting

Often leaders trying to figure out how to lead double or half-time can mistake a follower who simply doesn't like double-time, for something being wrong in their leading.

It's worth bearing in mind if your partner

doesn't seem to be comfortable dancing at the same speed as you, they may simply not have a natural tendency towards the timing you're trying to lead.

Likewise for followers adding double-time taps, you'll find it's just easier with some leaders than others. This has nothing to do with how well you're doing it.

Half-time is a sincopación because it skips some of the odd beats.

Summary

- Some dancers like to go fast and will lose their balance if you go slowly. Others prefer to go slowly and start to trip over themselves if you go fast.

- Half-time : As double-time is twice as fast, "half time" is half as fast.

- "Step at half-speed" is much easier than doing the associated maths with the counts

- Walking in half-time tends to feel awkward

- When trying to figure out how to lead double or half-time, don't mistake a follower who simply doesn't like double-time, for there being something wrong in your leading.

- Half-time is a sincopación because it skips some of the odd beats.

Chapter 4 Dinámica

"A good dancer is one who listens to the music...
We dance the music not the steps. You see, we are
painters. We paint the music with our feet."

Carlos Gavito

"Al Compás del Corazón" or "The beat of the heart" is a useful training wheel. But there's a lot of information crammed into that seemingly simple phrase.

For now, let's go with:

"The heartbeat is a metaphor for the beat of the music"

– sometimes it races, sometimes it skips a beat. Sometimes it stops altogether.

Like many of the songs, the dancer's relationship, in this case with the beat, is a more tempestuous one. Sometimes they are madly in love, slavishly following it. But at other times, they stray, lured by the siren call of the vocals and the instruments.

Sometimes they're ahead, sometimes behind. At other times, they seem to be drunkenly staggering around with no rhyme or reason.

Cuddle-shuffling

For this section I'm going to strongly recommend cuddle-shuffling. Yes, the tango walk shows off all these concepts incredibly well, but it's also a lot harder to do, let alone use a method for learning musicality. Starting with cuddle-shuffling and then graduating to walking will accelerate your learning and be a lot less stressful.

(Look, I stopped asking you to drink, so now it's cuddle-shuffling, just go with it. Or, y'know, drink while cuddle-shuffling...)

In Argentine Tango, there are five Dinámica – Stacato, Legato, Yum, Elastic and Raindrops.

Terminology – Dinámica

"Different ways of moving to accent the music"

Staccato

This is what most people think of as dancing on the beat. You may hear staccato music referred to as "Boom-boom" or "Thud-thud" music. Canaro's Invierno is a good example.

Probably the easiest way to think of dancing in a staccato way is to try to land flat-footed. This is still with your weight towards the front of your foot – but you want to avoid rolling your foot as you land.

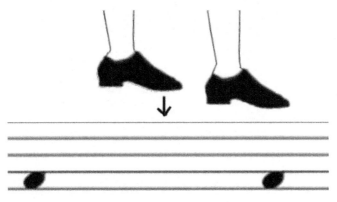

Think of it like a karate expert breaking bricks, or a drumbeat. There's an instant of impact.

It's very effective for dancing double-time.

Terminology - Staccato

"Sharp, crisp movements or sounds"

The angry, sharp movements often seen when Dancing with the Stars perform an Argentine Tango exemplify staccato movement.

Legato

At the other end of the spectrum is what most people think of as dancing to the melody. Search video sharing websites for "Vaughan Williams Lark Ascending" and you'll hear something with no beats at all.

But again, Legato goes deeper than that, embodying soft, fluid movements. It's Tai chi to staccato's karate.

It excels at dancing half-time.

Terminology - Legato

Rather than staccato's two bricks, Legato is two pillows colliding.

To step in a legato way, you want to roll your foot with each step. Stretch the moment out. If staccato is a series of snapshots, legato is a movie clip.

However, this presents a problem.

With staccato, you simply land on the beat. But with legato, do you land on the beat and then roll your foot? Or should you land ahead of the beat and finish rolling your foot on the beat? Or something in-between?

The short answer is you usually want to finish rolling your foot on the beat. If you're used to a more staccato dancing style, this can feel strange. If you dance "heel-first" as your heel now needs to land ahead of the beat, so that you complete the rolling step on the beat.

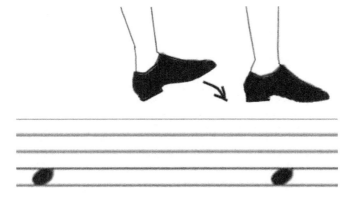

If you dance toe first, the toe needs to land ahead of the beat

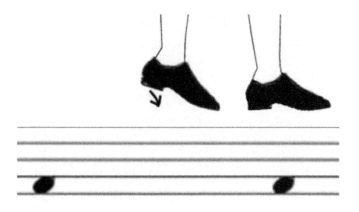

In both cases, you also need to take into account the extra time needed to complete the step and transfer your weight.

One way that can help make it feel more natural is to focus on completing your change of weight on the beat. Roll your foot, but at each beat, make sure that you are now able to cleanly and comfortably lift your free foot from the ground.

Troubleshooting

As a rule of thumb, if you watch a performance of Argentine Tango on Dancing with the Stars, or Strictly Come Dancing, if it's fast, then it's staccato. If it's slow, then it's legato.

Argentine Tango does have other dinámica that are rarely seen (or noticed!) in SCD and DwtS, which we'll start to look at in the next chapter.

Dinámica vs Sincopación

The fundamental difference is that Dinámica are ways of stepping on or around the beat, whereas Sincopacións are about stepping on extra beats or missing some out. You can combine both, for example stacatto tends to go well with double-time and legatto with half-time.

Summary

- "The heartbeat is a metaphor for the beat of the music" - sometimes it races, sometimes it skips a beat. Sometimes it stops altogether.

- Cuddle-shuffling is a good way to become comfortable with the different Dinámica.

- Dinámica are "Different ways of moving to accent the music."

- In Argentine Tango, there are five Dinámica – Stacato, Legato, Yum, Elastic and Raindrops.

- Staccato - dancing on the beat, think Karate.

- Often easier to do flat-footed, with your weight transferred in that instant.

- Legato - dancing to the melody. Tai chi.

- Often easier to roll foot – but allow extra

time to fully complete step.

Chapter 5 There are no mistakes

"Like a serpent, coils around the waist, that is
going to break."
‾ *Asi Se Baila El Tango*

I'll let you into a secret. If you make a mistake in tango, just name it – preferably in Spanish - and pretend it was intentional. In fact, at this point, you probably want to check that someone hasn't beaten you to it; traspie means "trip" for a reason.

You landed on the beat and *then* rolled your foot? Well that's a syncopation. As long as you don't keep doing it with every step, congratulations, you're doing "musicality."

You kinda missed the beat entirely, but remembered to roll your foot? Hey that's *advanced* musicality! (Actually, it's really hard to do once you get the hang of dancing on the beat.)

Yum (pronounced Schum)

This is usually reserved for dancing to Pugliese, but you'll get away with it if you have the space for a

47

decent tango walk of more than a few steps.

Terminology - Yum

It's pronounced in a similar way to the noise that a light saber makes when it's swung. Google translate does a pretty good version.

Do a search for "Pugliese La Yumba". It's specifically designed to dance to the crashing beat that Pugliese uses. "La Yumba performance" with the name of a Villa Urquiza couple, such as Geraldine and Javier, should get you examples.

While I much prefer cuddle-shuffling for learning musicality, this is the exception to the rule as it was specifically built to produce the characteristic tango walk.

For Leaders

The step starts off staccato, ideally on an Odd beat of the Compás. *"SCH."*

If you're starting from collect, you'll probably find it easier to bend the knee of your free leg and let your heel raise.

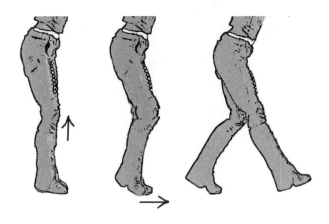

As you start to step, add a little push-off the rear foot to help you land flat-footed on your free foot. You'll probably find it easier to land with your weight towards the back of your foot.

Now it softens into legato as you transfer your weight to the front of your foot on the next beat of the Compás.

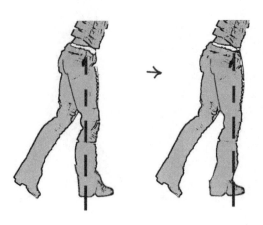

However, rather than fully collect your rear foot into another flat-footed step, leave it trailing out behind you with the heel raised - *"uuuuuuuuum."* This acknowledges the softer even beats in the tango Compás. In particular, for this walk, it's your knees that pass on the beat, not your feet.

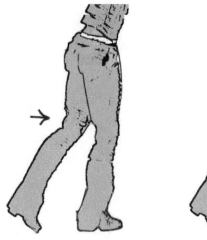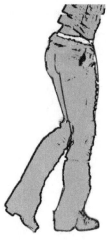

This leaves your trailing leg with the heel up ready to take the next step.

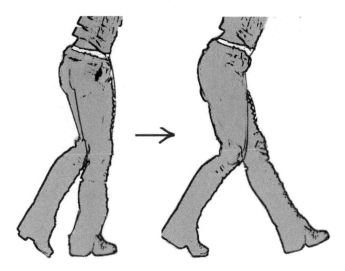

In doing, so your walk reflects the uneven heartbeat of tango's earlier Compás. Pugliese re-popularized this in 1946 as the "Golden Age" of tango music was ending.

The energy of each step is something like this:

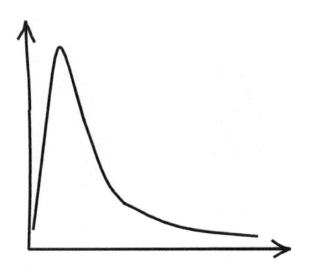

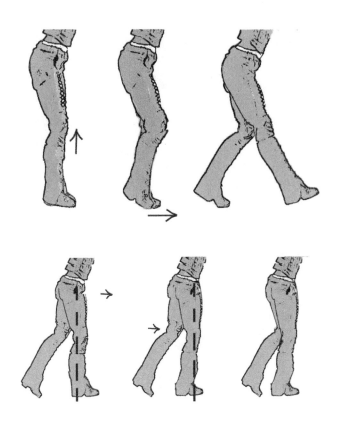

For Followers

"Ginger Rogers did everything (Fred Astaire) did backwards...and in high heels!" ~ Bob Thaves

The follower's version is basically the same as the leader's, just stepping backwards rather than forwards. A sharp initial step back, without rolling the foot and then smooth it out into legato finishing with the knees passing on the next beat.

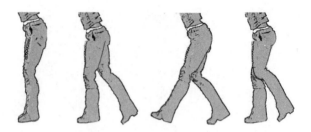

Because your knees come together on the beat, not your feet, this means your free foot is going to already be extended behind you, sometimes called "auto-projecting."

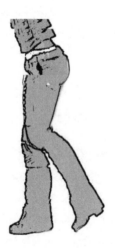

This isn't a "bad" thing, so much as a stylistic choice; some followers choose to always auto-project rather than collect.

Also, if you're wearing heels – or wearing flats but dancing with your heels off the ground - you'll probably prefer to keep your weight from going too far back into the heel area of the shoe. Instead, bend your knee more to allow the weight to stay forwards you travel backwards over the heel.

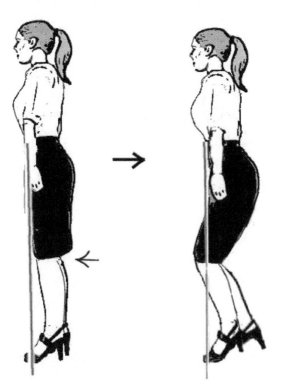

While you normally see this done as a tango walk with the leader going forwards and the follower backwards, there's nothing to stop the leader going sideways (sometimes seen at the beginning of performance to Pugliese) or backwards.

Likewise, as with all dinámica, this can be applied to other figures, such as boleos, beginning with a sharp staccato movement and then smoothing it out into legato.

Elastic

This takes the idea of Yum and applies it to a Slinky spring. Now you can freely mix in any combination of staccato and legato you like. For example, you could do the complete opposite of Yum, starting with legato and finishing with staccato.

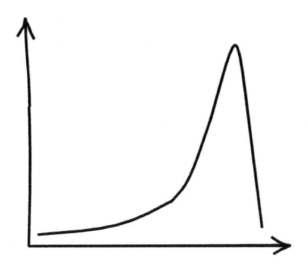

Trouble-shooting

A word of caution with this. Yum is a very specific combination that matches a core part of the tango Compás. I've seen elastic misunderstood as "slinging the different things together in random combinations."

I understand the appeal of this. As a leader it's hard to keep a lot of sequences in your head while you dance. The idea that you can simply walk, or indeed cuddle-shuffle, and just keep mixing together staccato and legato in different lengths means you have seemingly endless combinations –

your follower will never be bored!

The problem, is that they may well be confused instead.

Elastic opens up a wide range of possibilities, but it's then your job as a social dancer to chose the ones that actually make sense to the music at the time.

La Yumba is a good piece to experiment with this.

Exercise 5

Listen to La Yumba. Take a Yum step beginning as normal, with a staccato step on an odd beat, but then extend the legato part, taking 3 beats to collect your knees instead of 1.

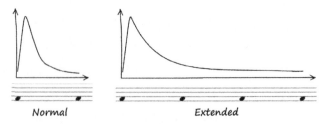

Normal   Extended

Summary

- Musicality covers a lot of "mistakes" in tango as long as you don't make them too often.

- Yum gives the characteristic tango walk.

- It begins with staccato and softening into legato.

- It's easier to do if you land flatfooted with your weight towards the back of your foot and then let it transfer through to the front of your foot.

- If following you may prefer to bend your supporting knee to keep your weight on the front of your foot.

- Elastic mixes and matches staccato and legato throughout a step or movement.

- However, it still needs to make sense with

the music being played at the time.

Chapter 6 Raindrops

"A chorus of raindrops will always sing for those who care to listen."

~ *Anthony T. Hincks*

Remember Goldilocks wanting her dancing speed "just right" while Papa and Baby Bear preferred something a bit different.

The same thing applies to Dinámica. Dancers who like to go slow, tend to like Legato; dancers who prefer to go fast, tend to like Stacatto.

Surprisingly, the biggest problem with Elastic, Yum and Raindrops, is simply whether your partner knows that they're allowed to dance this way.

But even then, different strokes for different folks.

If you try to dance these with someone they don't suit, it will be a lot harder. With Dinámica, it helps a lot to be compatible with each other.

"Raindrops keep falling on my head." ~ Burt Bacharach

The final Dinámic is based on the idea of raindrops falling pitter-patter all over the place, with a somewhat random feeling, but still somehow retaining the almost organic feel of rain falling. Put another way, it's syncopation.

Terminology - Raindrops

Instead of just stepping on every other beat, you mix it up.

Exercise 6

Listen to *Jamie Callum playing piano in "Don't stop the music."*

With a "normal" walk you might be stepping on the 1st, 3rd, 5th and 7th beat. Whereas when using raindrops, you might step on the 1st, 2nd, 4th, 7th and 8th instead.

Or whatever you want.

You can also step slightly ahead, or behind, the beat, rather than directly on it. Though again, ideally you're doing this because it makes some kind of sense to you in the music, rather than just for the sake of being random!

Exercise 7

Listen to "Rhapsody In Blue" by Gershwin and dance to it using the raindrops dynamic. There's definitely no right answer to this, so just have fun and mess around a bit.

Sam: 'Double pump?'

Mikaela: 'It squirts the fuel in so you can go faster'

Sam: 'Oh.... I like to go faster' ~ Transformers

I know a follower who likes to go fast.

Really fast!

And then she discovered the Raindrops Dinámic. (Which admittedly, I only have myself to blame, as I was the first one who led it on her.) While you don't have to do it fast – there's nothing wrong with the idea of raindrops randomly dripping down a window – when you crank the speed up, it makes milonga seem like a walk in a park.

With ice cream. On a gentle spring day.

This is why, frankly, it's really hard to criticize

musicality, because when you think about it, anything goes.

Try this to blow your mind in several stages...

Universal musicality

Open a video sharing website in two different tabs. In one, chose any tango performance you like. You can just type in "tango performance", or if you want some specific ideas, try "Carlitos and Noelia", "Sebastian Arce & Mariana Montes", or "Javier and Geraldine".

Once you've chosen one, press play and mute the sound. Now go to your second tab and type in a tango song. Again, if you're stuck for ides, try "Canaro Invierno", "DiSarli Bahia Blanca" or "Pugliese La Yumba". Press play, unmute it and switch back to the performance video.

Take a moment to think about this. You've chosen a random tango track and by now it's playing at a random point in the first performance.

Watch as the performers somehow still manage to display musicality to the song you chose. (It might take a moment for things to sync up, just count to ten.)

But we're not done yet. Now click on a random

point in the performance and see still more congruent musical interpretation! Next, try it out with the other musical suggestions.

How on earth are they able to demonstrate musicality to Canaro, DiSarli and Pugliese?

I mean, seriously, it doesn't get much more diverse than that! Feel free to try it with different performers and songs.

I'm not done blowing your mind yet, though.

Now try it with "Gotan Paris Texas". Yup, it works with nuevo too.

And finally try it with "Lindsey Stirling Crystallize", a dub-step hip-hop violinist!

When you've recovered from that, an exercise to consider is to take each of the above concepts, staccato, legato and so on, and find a piece of music you think exemplifies it. A lot of tango music will have more than one of type of Dinámica in it, so you might want to consider classical, hip hop, rap, jazz - whatever works for you.

The trick is to chose a piece of music that has a matching Beats per Minute or BPM. Usually an internet search for "Song title, Orchestra BPM" will tell you the relevant number eg "Poema Canaro BPM" is 117 and "Crystallize Lindsey Stirling BPM" is 140.

Up 'till now we've mainly considered musicality in terms of weight-changes and walking. But musicality can be expressed through your entire body; from sharp staccato boleos, to soft legato breath.

Put on some music you like and just try moving to it however you please. You might want to shrug your shoulder rhythmically, or do gentle hand movements. If you get stuck, try watching videos of other people dancing to it. Or find a video of someone conducting it and watch their hand movements.

Gabrielle Roth's 5 Rhythms videos are filled with ideas.

When that's starting to work for you, play around with actual tango movements. Feel what it's like to do an ocho, or a boleo in each of those different ways.

You may well find that you really don't like a number of Dinámica. That's ok. It's something to bear in mind when deciding if you want to dance to a certain piece of music or Orchestra that tends to favor that Dinámic.

Now put on some tango music and ask yourself

"What's going on in this piece?" Most tango music has more than one of these Dinámica in it. Again, move around with your shoulders, hands, tap your foot, whatever. Play around with it. Find where you can be soft and sharp and so on. Find the places where you can do both.

(Hint, try DiSarli's Bahia Blanca - "beginner's music", hah!)

Repeat, but with tango movements. At this point you might want to consider getting a helpful partner to go to a práctica with you and try this stuff out. Failing that, well, everyone else experiments in milongas anyway....

Summary

- The Raindrops dinámic is based on the idea of raindrops falling pitter-patter all over the place, with a somewhat random feeling, but still somehow retaining the almost organic feel of rain falling.

- It should still make sense with the music being played.

- But if you saw it being danced but couldn't hear the music, it would probably appear to be random.

- Good musicality is surprisingly robust.

- You can watch it being danced to different music entirely, even from another genre and usually as long as the BPM is the same, it will make sense.

Chapter 7 Rebounds - Rebotes

"The wonderful thing about tiggers

They're bouncy, trouncy, flouncy, pouncy

Fun, fun, fun, fun, fun!"

¯*Tigger*

One of the biggest problems with using Dinámica, is a reliance on sequences and moves. When you're trying to learn something new, the less pieces of the puzzle, or "moving parts", the better.

Rebounds, or rebotes (*reb-O-tes*), are surprisingly robust for dancing all the Dinámica. They also work rather nicely with cuddle-shuffling!

Terminology – Weight change

A weight change is supposed to be when you transfer your weight fully from one foot to the other.

Unfortunately, many leaders don't fully transfer

their own or their follower's weight when they do a weight change (See Book 4.)

Many tango movements are the result of mistakes that worked. If you are walking and someone suddenly steps into that space, the sensible thing is to either stop, or retreat.

In both cases, you have the option to continue with your original step immediately after.

These are the two basic versions of rebounds – "Footprints in the sand" and "Touch and go."

For simplicity, we'll focus on the rebound of a leader's forwards step, but the concept applies equally well to a back or side-step.

Rather than complete the step and fully transfer the follower's weight and collect their feet together - for example to avoid stepping into the couple who've just cut in front of you - instead, come to an early stop.

Footprints in the Sand

For this version, If you were dancing on sand, you would aim to make a nice deep, clear footprint. You can stretch out the movement as much as possible in the time given (lyrical). It's almost the opposite of "bouncy" - sorry, Tigger.

You may also choose to let your heel lower.

Notice that the follower isn't far back enough to properly complete the weight-change.

Now the follower's weight is properly transferred on to the standing foot. However, this still counts as a rebound, and is often how "footprints in the sand" end up. The distinction is that the follower's free foot doesn't come into collect next to their other foot, ie avoid this.

As a leader, to keep the follower stretching out a movement, keep in movement yourself.

You can also do this rebound multiple times; it may suit the music, or perhaps the couple in front of you are taking a while to move away. Especially keep your free foot in motion and be able to take it cleanly of the ground. If you can't take it off the ground, your partner's free leg may not be as free as you think.

"Touch and Go"

Think of this as almost a tap. As you take each step you want to choose a more staccato approach. Minimize the movement of your heel as you land, keeping it at the same height as much as possible, moving it more like a tripod formed by your inner instep and ball of your foot.

If you were dancing on sand, you'd leave as small as impression as possible with the foot you're rebounding on. This can often mean not transferring much weight onto the foot. This staccato version has a feeling of cracking a whip, it's a very light, quick reversal.

It works well as a retreat back to a collect.

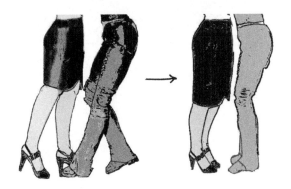

The leader can also augment the lead using their closed-side hand to stop and then pull the follower towards them. This is especially effective when avoiding collisions. Followers can also "lead" this if they see their leader's stepping backwards into another couple. It's important to stress that you use your closed-side hand to signal danger to your partner, rather than physically yanking them.

Summary

- Rebounds, or rebotes (reb-O-tes), are surprisingly robust for dancing all the Dinámica. They also work rather nicely with cuddle-shuffling!

- There are the two basic versions of rebounds

- "Footprints in the sand" - If you were dancing on sand, you would aim to make a nice deep, clear footprint.

- "Touch and go." - almost a tap

- Rather than complete the step and fully transfer the follower's weight to a collect, instead come to an early stop.

- As a leader, to keep the follower stretching out a movement, keep in movement yourself.

- The leader can also augment the lead using

their closed-side hand to stop and then pull the follower towards them. This is especially effective when avoiding collisions.

- Followers can also "lead" this if they see their leader's stepping backwards into another couple.

Chapter 8 Rocksteps – La Cadencia

"Just find what works for you, what style suits you best, and just be confident enough to rock it."

¯Odell Beckham, Jr.

The other thing I like about rebounds is that, like cuddle-shuffling, they're very effective at dancing in small spaces. On a crowded floor, you can dance musically with just the space you physically need for your embrace. Compare that with the average space needed for a sequence.

This also massively reduces the amount of stress involved.

Imagine being safely cuddled up to someone, dancing small musical steps in place. The flow of dancing around the floor has ground to a halt because it's so overcrowded. In the space of a three minute song, you're going to move about ten feet.

If you're lucky.

Only, you don't care, because you don't need any more space than floor that's under your feet.

Meanwhile, the leaders around you are going through their "Big Book of Sequences" trying to work out how to lead any of them when they all need at least six feet of movement. And if they somehow manage to get one to work, then they feel obliged to move onto a different one so their follower doesn't get bored.

Instead, you and your follower are just playing in the moment with the music.

While you could just use weight-changes, rebounds open up your musical possibilities a lot. And they in turn have several variations.

One variation of a rebound is the rock-step or cadencia (*ca-Den-cia*).

Rock-steps are essentially two rebounds cut in half and stuck together. The beginning is the same as a rebound, but then you immediately go back into a rebound in the opposite direction.

For example, you might start by leading the follower into a rebound on her back-step, partly transfer their weight back towards you. But then you rebound off your own back foot (as if the follower had led a rebound on you.) At this point, you're both now heading in the original direction – the follower is taking a back-step.

In essence, you're just partially transferring your weight; then rock back and forth without completely transferring your weight to either foot.

Again, you can chose whether to use footprints in the sand, or touch and go as shown here.

"Touch and go" rock-steps are great for staccato double-times, especially when you don't have much space around you. What's important here is not to move that much. It's a slight back and forth action. Because you're trying to go at double-time, smaller is better.

"Footprints in the sand" works well for legato rock-steps.

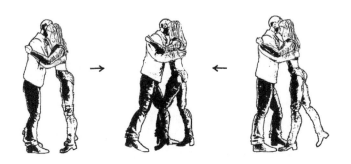

And you can mix them up, for example using Elastic to start with a legato footprint in the sand, rocking back into a staccato touch and go.

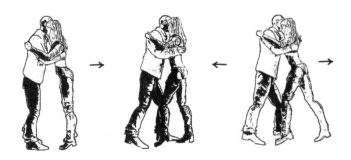

Hesitations

You can also lead any step as a series of smaller steps. It's easier to lead if you lower slightly on each hesitation.

There's two distinct ways to lead hesitations.

The first is similar to a rock-step You take a small step forwards, allow the follower to push off the ground, then rock back enough so that their free leg is once again able to move. Now lead a slightly bigger and lower step.

Doing this three times tends to feel right, but there's no specific rule. Just be aware that the further you go, the harder it will become to take the next part of the hesitation.

Drop steps

You should definitely practice these in flats first, especially for back-steps. You might also want to have your hand against a wall for balance.

Take a small step forwards. Keep your weight mainly on your back foot. Say an 80% / 20% split between your back and forward feet.

All you're going to do is lift your front foot up slightly. You might find it's easier to bend your knee. You will almost immediately fall forwards.

Because, gravity.

Let your front foot land back on the floor. This doesn't have to be a particularly big step.

Troubleshooting

Again, some people will find it easier to lift their foot a small amount, others will prefer a larger movement. Do whatever's most comfortable for you.

The important detail is that unlike the rock-step, you don't need to shift your weight back, like this.

In the 80/20 position your front leg is stopping you falling. If you take it away, you'll naturally fall forwards. Just remember to keep a tango posture as you do it, rather than leaning over like this.

With each drop-step in the hesitation, you'll find that more of your weight is on now your front foot.

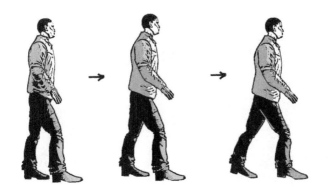

You don't need to micro-manage where your front foot lands. Your body has years of experience with this.

Repeat until you can do it comfortably.

You can also do them to the side or backwards. The technique is the same whether you're leading or following.

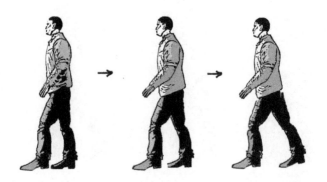

Though as a follower, if you want to keep the heel of your front foot off the ground during a back-step, bend the knee of you front leg.

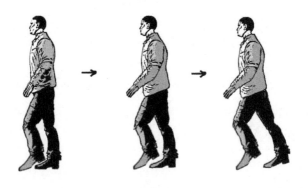

Indeed, you can use hesitations to break-up any movement from sacadas to boleos.

Combinations

You can also add a rock-step partway through a hesitation step before completing it.

And again you can use which ever musicality you feel suits the music.

Projections

Projections don't involve any transfer of weight. The follower is led to extend or "project" their free leg.

But otherwise, it can be done with any Dominic or sincopación. And it can also be done in a series of hesitations, though without the need for the follower's free foot to touch / rebound off the floor on each one. As a style point, some follower may add a small tap, to mark the hesitation and whatever it (hopefully) corresponds to in the music.

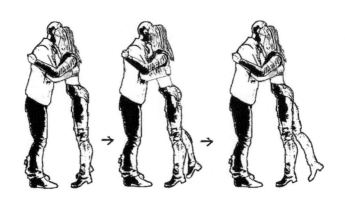

Summary

- Rock-steps are essentially two rebounds cut in half and stuck together.

- "Touch and go" rock-steps are great for staccato double-times

- "Footprints in the sand" works well for legato rock-steps.

- You can mix them up, for example using Elastic to start with a legato footprint in the sand, rocking back into a staccato touch and go.

- You can also use Hesitations to lead any step as a series of smaller steps.

- It's easier to lead if you lower slightly on each hesitation.

- You can either use a rock-step or a drop-step.

- Projections don't involve any transfer of

weight. The follower is led to extend or "project" their free leg.

- They can be done with any dinámic or sincopación and can also be done in a series of hesitations.

Chapter 9 The Lead

"Oh my God, Persephone how could you do this? You betrayed me."

"Cause and Effect, my love."
"Cause? There is no cause for this. What cause?"
"What cause? How about the lipstick you're still wearing?"

- Persephone and Merovingian

What is the lead for a rebound, anyway?

What specifically is it that directs the follower to touch the floor and then push off it? How are they supposed to know what the leader actually wants and when? Especially with the different variations.

Well first, we need to see things from the follower's point of view.

Exercise 8

Start in flats. Step backwards until your belt buckle would be behind the heel of your front leg.

Now, without moving your belt buckle forwards, try to lift your rear leg off the ground.

If you managed to do that briefly (probably by concentrating on bending the knee of your rear leg), now try to hold your rear foot off the ground. If you can do that, then James Randi may be interested in offering you $1,000,000 for your supernatural ability to levitate!

Belt buckles

So if you want to lead the follow to do a rebound, move their belt buckle behind their front heel and stop. Gravity will take care of the rest. If you want a bigger step, just lead a bigger step before you stop. Again, gravity is your friend once you get their belt buckle past their standing foot.

For followers, it's important to recognize when you've reached this point, so you know you're no longer projecting and will probably need to put your foot down when you stop moving.

The other important subtlety for followers is a style choice. Some follower's prefer not to put their heels down when stepping backwards. But once your belt buckle goes behind your front foot, your natural instinct is to put the heel of your front foot down. If you're in flats, this also causes a rather sudden loss of height.

To get around this, bend the knee of your front leg. This in turn will lift the heel more, letting you keep your heels off the ground throughout the rebound and indeed, back-steps in general.

Again it's a stylistic choice, but as a follower, if you started with a "straight" leg (the knee should still be soft), then bending your knee will lower you unless you raise your heels by the same amount. Another solution is to keep your knees bent when you collect. It also effectively prevents the leader from putting you back onto your heels as you're already in a bent knee / heel up position.

You'll still lower slightly for longer steps, but the leader will expect that – and most likely will also be lowering slightly themselves as they also take a longer step.

Sidesteps

For sidesteps, you want to move the follower's belt buckle past the outside of where the follower's free leg was when it was collected.

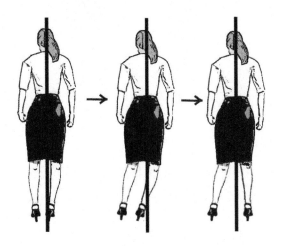

The middle step in the above illustration is just to clarify where the belt buckle is. In practice, the follower would look more like this.

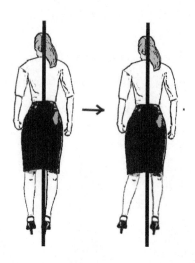

In essence, move their belt buckle to where you want it to be. For a longer step, move it further.

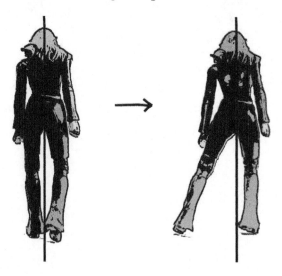

For forward steps, move the belt buckle past the toes of their supporting leg.

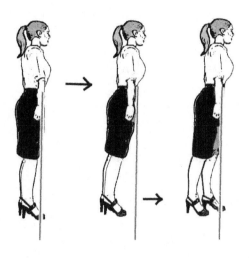

Again, for a larger step, move it further.

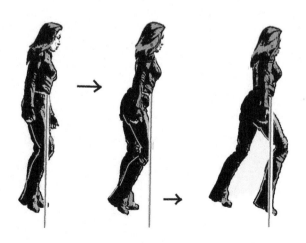

Projections

For projections, simply use smaller movements that don't take the follower to the point where gravity forces them to put their foot down.

If you want to make the projection bigger, lower your follower. In close embrace it's fine to let the follower slide down the leader's torso, rather, than the leader bending over and compromising their posture.

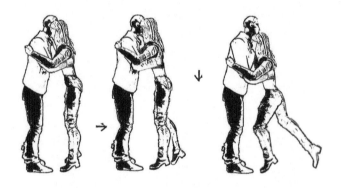

You will see performances where the leader does bend over, but this is for a specific visual aesthetic.

Troubleshooting

Be aware that some clothes, especially skirts and dresses can restrict the size of steps, especially side-steps. There's a reason skirts like this are popular among some followers, other than the visual aesthetic.

Summary

- To lead a rebound, move their belt buckle behind their front heel and stop. Gravity will take care of the rest.

- If you want a bigger step, just lead a bigger step before you stop.

- For followers, it's important to recognize when you've reached this point, so you know you're no longer projecting and will probably need to put your foot down when you stop moving.

- As a follower you can bend your knee and lift your heel to prevent your weight going back onto your heels.

- Lifting your heels will lessen the effect of you from lowering as you step.

- For sidesteps, you want to move the follower's belt buckle past the outside of where the follower's free leg was when it was collected.

- For forward steps, move the belt buckle past the toes of their supporting leg.

- In essence, move their belt buckle to where you want it to be. For a longer step, move it further.

- Be mindful of clothing and any restrictions it may place on you or your partner's movement.

- For projections, simply use smaller movements that don't take the follower to the point where gravity forces them to put their foot down.

- If you want to make the projection bigger, lower your follower.

Epilogue

"He who knows others is wise; he who knows himself is enlightened."

—*Lao Tzu*

I remember dancing at a Práctica in the upstairs of a bar. There were a couple visiting the city from another country and so naturally I asked the lady to dance to make her feel welcome.

We danced a simple musical dance. Using some of the Dinámica, we did different rebounds, walking and weight-changes.

That was pretty much it.

At the end, she looked up at me with a big smile and exclaimed "Yes! That's it exactly! Please explain it to my husband" and started to lead me to him. He'd seen us dance, heard her and now had the look of a condemned man.

I smiled and said

"You saw me dancing with her?"

He nodded.

"And you know that's what she wants to do?"

He nodded again.

"But you're in that place right now, where you really want to learn the cool moves. Once you've done that, then you'll be happy to dance like I just did."

The look on his face changed to one of "Finally, somone understands me!"

"Yes, that's it exactly!" he replied.

I smiled at her "It's just a phase he needs to go through. Just be patient, it'll be worth it."

Not quite the outcome she was hoping for...

Learning Argentine Tango is a balancing act. Cuddle-shuffling will get you where you want to go much faster, especially with musicality. And for some dancers, cuddle-shuffling with rebounds and musicality is as far as they need to go to be happily covered in pixie dust at the end of the night.

But if you want to learn the cool stuff, or why DiSarli wore sunglasses, then you should do that too. Tango should be something that makes you happy - or at least gives you some sense of accomplishment for the more angst-ridden among you!

And while **learning** cool moves tends to be a phase, **dancing** them is definitely one of the paths to happiness in Argentine Tango. There may well come a point where cuddle-shuffling has taken you as far as you can go with it.

As for Argentine Tango itself. I often feel it's like trying to drink the ocean – no matter how long I dance, there's always new insights and experiences. Becoming a Good Social Dancer is a lot like finally reaching the top of the mountain, only to see a vast new landscape on the other side for you to explore.

But as climbing that mountain can take years, I strongly recommend you try to enjoy it!

Oliver Kent, Spring 2019

Terminology

Normal time

The baseline for tango – roughly one step per second.

Double time

If you're going "twice as fast" as a normal tango walk it's called "Double time." - roughly two steps per second and walking on each beat of the Compás

Half time

As double-time is twice as fast, "half time" is half as fast.

Dinámica

"Different ways of moving to accent the music"

Staccato

"Sharp, crisp movements or sounds"

Legato

Rather than staccato's two bricks, Legato is two pillows colliding.

Yum

It's the same noise that a light saber makes when it's swung.
Schummmmmmmm.

Raindrops

Instead of just stepping on every other beat, you mix it up.

Terminology: Sincopación

When you're not marching to the beat.

Weight change

A weight change is supposed to be when you transfer your weight fully from one foot to the other.

Printed in Great Britain
by Amazon